the Country Friends Collection™

Main Dishes

Kate
... knows what wieners are made of and likes 'em anyway.

Mary Elizabeth
... owns 53 different aprons & 117 potholders.

Holly
... loves cooking for a crowd.

It ain't a fit night out for man or beast

— W.C. Fields

Let the North Wind blow!

What care we?

We'll warm up in no time with a big old plate-full of this old-fashioned meal!

Kate's Beef and Noodles

2 LB. BEEF CHUCK, CUBED
1 CLOVE GARLIC, MINCED
1 C. ONION, CHOPPED
1/2 C. CELERY, CHOPPED
6 TO 8 CUPS WATER

3 BEEF BOUILLON CUBES
1/8 t. THYME
8 OZ. PKG. WIDE NOODLES
SALT & PEPPER TO TASTE

Spray Dutch oven with cooking spray. Brown beef with garlic, onion & celery. Add water, bouillon & thyme to beef mixture; bring to a boil. Cover & simmer 1 1/2 to 2 hours. Skim & discard foam that accumulates. Bring pot back to a boil and add noodles — cook according to package directions. Salt & pepper to taste. ③

Serve with a green salad & hot rolls — delicious!

Truck-Patch Stew with Dumplings

Kate's Grand Daddy had a truck-patch ~ a garden of all sorts of delicious vegetables. Once a week, baskets of produce were loaded into the truck and toted to town to market. This recipe uses all kinds of farm-fresh veggies ...and reminds Kate of her Grand Daddy.

Stew:

- 2 LBS. lean beef stew meat, cut in 1" cubes
- 1 large onion, cut in chunks
- 4 large carrots, cut in ½" pieces
- 4 medium potatoes, peeled & cut into 1" cubes
- 3 stalks celery, cut in 1" pieces
- 2 T. quick-cooking tapioca
- ½ to 1 t. dried thyme, crushed
- 1 t. salt
- ½ t. pepper
- 2 cloves garlic, minced
- 1 T. instant beef bouillon
- 2 · 16 oz. cans diced tomatoes
- 3/4 cup water
- 1 T. brown sugar
- 2 fresh ears of corn, cut in 2" slices
- 10 oz. pkg. frozen peas, thawed

PEA PATCH

4

QUICK & EASY Dumplings:

2 c. Packaged Biscuit Mix
1/4 t. poultry seasoning
2/3 c. milk

HowTo : Layer beef stew meat in bottom of a large roasting pan. (with this recipe, there's no need to brown the meat.) Top meat with onions, carrots, potatoes & celery. Sprinkle tapioca, thyme, salt, pepper, garlic & bouillon over veggies. Add diced tomatoes, water & brown sugar. Cover & bake for 2½ hours in 325° oven, stirring occasionally. Add corn. Cover & bake an additional 1 to 1½ hours 'til meat & veggies are tender. Remove from oven. On stove top at low heat, stir in peas.

Prepare dumplings by combining the ingredients in a mixing bowl 'til moistened. Drop dumpling dough on top of bubbling stew. Simmer uncovered for 10 minutes. Cover & simmer an additional 10 minutes.

Serves 6-8.

Kids Love

CHILI OLÉ!

On a crisp autumn afternoon, load up the thermos with chili, throw in some lunch-size bags of corn chips to use as bowls, shredded cheddar cheese and plastic spoons.

Take a hike in the woods then enjoy this portable picnic!

(Make sure you have enough for seconds.)

CRISPY CORN CHIPS

YUMMY GOOD!

CHILI OLÉ Ingredients ~

~ AND INSTRUCTIONS

3 LBS. LEAN GROUND BEEF
2 MED. ONIONS, CHOPPED
2 CLOVES GARLIC, MINCED
1 LG. GREEN PEPPER,
       CHOPPED

3 TO 4 t. CHILI POWDER
1 BAY LEAF
2 · 16 OZ. CANS WHOLE
   TOMATOES, CHOPPED
8 OZ. CAN TOMATO SAUCE
6 OZ. CAN TOMATO PASTE
WATER
1 t. CUMIN
1 T. SUGAR
3 · 16 OZ. CANS RED
     KIDNEY BEANS

IN LARGE SAUCEPAN OR DUTCH OVEN, BROWN BEEF. DRAIN FAT. ADD ONION, GARLIC & GREEN PEPPER TO PAN ~ SAUTE 3 MINUTES. STIR IN CHILI POWDER, CUMIN, SUGAR, BAY LEAF, TOMATOES, TOMATO SAUCE, TOMATO PASTE & 2 PASTE CANS OF WATER. SIMMER, COVERED, FOR 1 HOUR. STIR OCCASIONALLY. REMOVE BAY LEAF AND ADD BEANS. COOK, COVERED, FOR ADDT'L 30 MINUTES.

(SERVES 6 TO 8)

CHILI OLÉ TOPPER IDEAS ...

 I Like Monterrey Jack Cheese. — Mary Elizabeth —

Mmm!! Chopped Onions! — Kate —

 A big dollop of Sour Cream! — Holly ~

 Crunched Up & Smooshed Crackers! — Molly —

 Corn Chips are great. — BUD —

 Grblx ma Bleck! — skeeter ~

 Milk Bones. — Spotty ~

Use YOUR IMAGINATION!

MOM'S Spaghetti WITH MEAT-BALLS!

* A FAMILY FAVORITE, ESPECIALLY WITH THE YOUNGER GENERATION !

A child
Should always s
what's true

And speak when
he is spoken to

And behave
mannerly at tal

At least as far
as he is able.

—Robert Louis
Stevenson—

HOW TO MAKE THE MEATBALLS:

* FIX A DOUBLE BATCH! BAKE MEATBALLS ACCORDING TO THE RECIPE...FREEZE INDIVIDUALLY ON COOKIE SHEET... PACKAGE IN FREEZER CONTAINER 'TIL LATER!

1 LB. Lean Ground Beef
½ LB. Italian Sausage
⅔ c. Italian-seasoned bread crumbs
1 onion, chopped   ½ t. salt
½ c. milk   ⅛ t. pepper
1 egg
1 T. Parmesan cheese, grated

Combine all ingredients in a large mixing bowl 'til well blended then shape into 1½" balls. Place meatballs in ungreased 13"x9" baking dish. Bake uncovered at 375° for 20 minutes or until meatballs are light brown. Drain off fat, and pour sauce over meatballs. Cover pan ~ bake at 350° for 30 to 45 minutes. Serve over cooked spaghetti.

MOM'S SPECIAL SAUCE:

1 med. onion, chopped   1 c. water
2 cloves garlic, chopped   ⅓ c. dry red wine
1 green pepper, chopped   1 t. sugar
1 T. olive oil   1 t. oregano
14½ oz. can diced tomatoes
8 oz. can tomato sauce   ½ t. basil
6 oz. can tomato paste
4½ oz. jar of mushrooms, sliced

In a big pot, cook onion, garlic & green pepper in olive oil 'til tender. Add remaining ingredients to pot. Cover & simmer 1 hour. Now it's ready to pour over the meatballs. Dig in!

Creamed Chipped Beef

★ **BASIC RECIPE:**

4 oz. CHIPPED DRIED BEEF   2 T. FLOUR
2 T. BUTTER OR MARGARINE   1½ C. MILK

★ **OPTIONAL INGREDIENTS, AS HER ROYALNESS SO WISHES:**

1 TO 2 T. MINCED ONION   1 T. DRY SHERRY
1 TO 2 T. GREEN PEPPER,   DASH WORCHESTERSHIRE SAUCE
   FINELY CHOPPED
¼ C. MUSHROOMS, SLICED
   WITH A DASH OF NUTMEG

★ **GARNISH, AS DIRECTED BY HER HIGHNESS:**

CHOPPED PARSLEY & CHIVES   PAPRIKA

CUT CHIPPED DRIED BEEF INTO SMALL
PIECES. MELT BUTTER OR MARGARINE IN SAUCEPAN.
ADD CHIPPED DRIED BEEF (INCLUDING ANY
OPTIONAL INGREDIENTS) ~ SAUTÉ 2 TO 3 MINUTES.
SPRINKLE FLOUR OVER MIXTURE & BLEND WELL.
STIRRING CONSTANTLY, ADD MILK ALL AT
ONCE & SIMMER 'TIL THICKENED. SPOON
OVER HOT BUTTERED TOAST, MASHED OR
BAKED POTATO. GARNISH.

Fit for a Queen!

HER ROYAL ROYALNESS IN HOLLY

10

Homestyle Pot Roast
with Vegetables

You'll need:

3 to 4 LB. BEEF POT ROAST
ALL-PURPOSE FLOUR
2 T. OIL
SALT & PEPPER TO TASTE
½ c. BEEF BROTH
¼ c. RED WINE

8 OZ. WHOLE MUSHROOMS, HALVED
¼ t. THYME, CRUSHED
2 CLOVES GARLIC, FINELY CHOPPED
1 MEDIUM ONION, SLICED
4 POTATOES, QUARTERED
5 CARROTS, CUT IN 2" PIECES

(SERVES 6 TO 8)

TRIM FAT FROM ROAST. COAT ALL SIDES OF MEAT WITH FLOUR. IN A DUTCH OVEN, HEAT OIL & BROWN ROAST ON ALL SIDES. SPRINKLE WITH SALT & PEPPER. ADD BROTH, WINE, THYME, GARLIC & ONIONS. COVER & BAKE IN 325° OVEN FOR 1¼ – 1½ HOURS. ADD TATERS, CARROTS & MUSHROOMS. COVER & CONTINUE BAKING ANOTHER 30 TO 45 MINUTES 'TIL MEAT & VEGGIES ARE TENDER. PLACE ON OVEN-PROOF PLATTER & KEEP WARM ⁓ NOW FIX

☆ No-Lumps Gravy ☆

FOR PERFECT GRAVY EVERY SINGLE TIME!

½ c. VEGETABLE OR CANOLA OIL
FLOUR

1 t. BOTTLED BROWNING SAUCE

POUR OIL IN MIXING BOWL. ADDING SMALL AMOUNT FLOUR AT A TIME, WHISK OIL & FLOUR 'TIL MIXTURE IS CONSISTENCY OF HONEY. ADD TO HOT PAN DRIPPINGS OR BROTH TO MAKE GRAVY ⁓ SIMMER 'TIL THICK. ADD BROWNING SAUCE (A LITTLE GOES A LONG WAY ⁓ TOO MUCH WILL RESULT IN A BITTER TASTE!). ADD SMALL AMOUNT OF BROTH IF GRAVY GETS TOO THICK.

Hearty

So good, you'll want to

Mix all ingredients together reserving 1/4 c. chili sauce for later use.

1 1/2 LB. Lean Ground Beef
1/2 LB. Lean Pork or Sausage
1/2 c. onion, chopped
1/4 c. Green Pepper, chopped
1 egg
3/4 c. Quick-Cooking Oats
1/2 c. milk
3/4 c. Chili Sauce, divided
1 T. steak Sauce
1/2 t. Salt
1/4 t. pepper

Kiss the Cook

12

meatloaf

make 2 ~ one for supper & one for sandwiches tomorrow!

Place mixture into an ungreased loaf pan or round casserole dish, and spoon reserved chili sauce over top.

Bake, uncovered, in a 350° oven for 1 - 1¼ hours. Drain off fat. Cool in pan 5 to 10 minutes for easier slicing. Remove from pan, slice and serve.

IT WILL CURE WHAT AILS YOU.

MARY ELIZABETH'S GRANDMA'S MOST·BESTEST CHICKEN SOUP

2 CHICKEN BREASTS
6 c. WATER
1/2 c. CELERY, FINELY CHOPPED
1/2 c. ONION, FINELY CHOPPED
1/2 c. CARROTS, SLICED

4 c. CHICKEN BROTH
1 c. FINE NOODLES OR EGG PASTINA

1/8 t. POULTRY SEASONING
SALT & PEPPER TO TASTE

GRANDMA'S INSTRUCTIONS

Honey, reach up on that tall shelf and get that big old pan for me — Grandma's too short to reach. Now, put the chicken breasts & water in the pan and cover it — put it on the stove to boil. Careful! That stove'll burn your little fingers. Is it simmerin'? All-righty, now just let it simmer. Let's skim off that foam from the top & sides of the pan. Okey-dokey — let's go out on the porch & let that cook about 45 minutes. By then, that old meat will slide right off the bone!

Sweetie, take the chicken out of the pot and let it cool, and I'll skim that bad old fat off the broth. Now, take all those veggies & some extra broth and add it to the chicken stock in the pot. Did you know your great-aunt Edna gave me that pot back in '36? We'll just let that all simmer about, oh, 15 minutes then we'll bring it back to a boil. Now we'll add the noodles.... you take the chicken off the bone and chop it up. Just throw out the bones & skin, honey. OK — shall we add a pinch of seasoning now? Don't burn your tongue! This will make a nice lunch for you, me & your 2 cousins Mimi & Ellis.

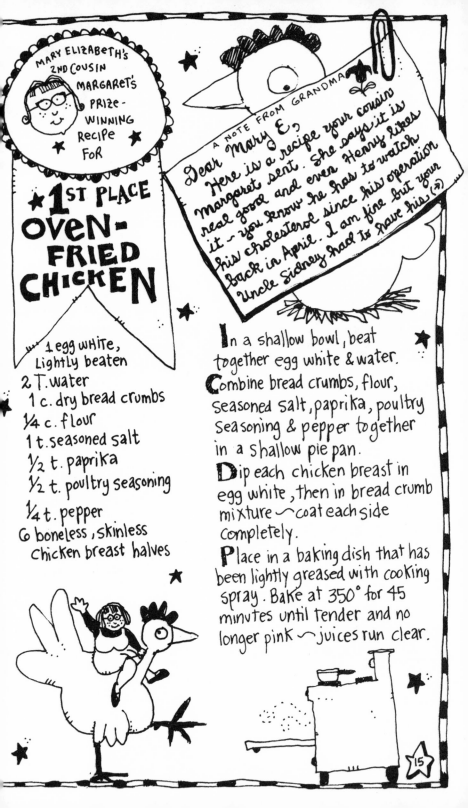

MARY ELIZABETH's 2ND COUSIN MARGARET'S PRIZE-WINNING RECIPE FOR

★1ST PLACE OVEN-FRIED CHICKEN

A NOTE FROM GRANDMA

Dear Mary E.,

Here is a recipe your cousin Margaret sent. She says it is real good and even Henry likes it — you know he has to watch his cholesterol since his operation back in April. I am fine but your Uncle Sidney had to have his (→)

1 egg white, lightly beaten
2 T. water
1 c. dry bread crumbs
¼ c. flour
1 t. seasoned salt
½ t. paprika
½ t. poultry seasoning
¼ t. pepper
6 boneless, skinless chicken breast halves

In a shallow bowl, beat together egg white & water.

Combine bread crumbs, flour, seasoned salt, paprika, poultry seasoning & pepper together in a shallow pie pan.

Dip each chicken breast in egg white, then in bread crumb mixture — coat each side completely.

Place in a baking dish that has been lightly greased with cooking spray. Bake at 350° for 45 minutes until tender and no longer pink — juices run clear.

15

Where our work is, there let our JOY be.

~ Tertullian (c.160-240)

Menu!

Stuffed Turkey Tenderloins with Orange Cranberry Glaze

Savory Mashed Potatoes

Pumpkin Pie

Stuffed Turkey Tenderloins

the taste of Thanksgiving, all in one dish! Give thanks!

2 turkey tenderloins, about 1½ pounds each,
plus **1** package herb-seasoned stuffing mix or your favorite stuffing recipe

Slice each tenderloin lengthwise, cutting almost to but not through opposite side. Open each tenderloin like a book, forming two large rectangles. Pound meat to about ½" thickness. Prepare stuffing mix according to directions for stuffing a turkey. Spoon stuffing mixture evenly down center of one piece of meat, and top with remaining pieces. Tie securely with heavy white cotton string at 1½" intervals, slightly overlapping sides to hold in stuffing. Place in shallow roasting pan & cover with lid or foil. Bake at 325° for 1 - 1¼ hours. Baste in glaze (recipe next page) during last 30 minutes. Garnish with orange slices.

Make dinner a Group Effort!

(and let the men do the dishes)

17

Orange Cranberry Glaze

A delicious sauce to use with Stuffed Turkey Tenderloins

- 1 T. cornstarch
- ¼ t. salt
- ⅛ t. cinnamon
- 1 t. brown sugar
- 4 T. orange juice, divided
- ½ c. whole cranberry sauce
- 2 T. margarine

Blend together cornstarch, salt, cinnamon & 2 tablespoons orange juice in small bowl and set aside. Combine remaining orange juice, cranberry sauce & margarine in saucepan. Stirring constantly, heat until cranberry sauce melts. Blend in cornstarch mixture. Continue to stir until mixture thickens & boils. Remove from heat. Glaze if ready to use.
* If mixture's too thick, add 1 teaspoon of orange juice at a time. 18

A man hath no better thing under the sun than to **Eat**, and to **Drink**, and to **Be Merry.**

— The Bible
Ecclesiastes 8:15

"We hath no better thing to eat under the sun than these mashed potatoes." —Kate

Savory Mashed Potatoes

5 large potatoes, peeled & diced

¼ c. milk

½ t. seasoned salt

3 T. margarine

1 c. sour cream

3 oz. package cream cheese, softened

1 t. dried chives

½ c. butter-flavored crackers, crushed

¼ c. cheddar cheese, shredded

Cook potatoes in salted water 'til tender ~ drain. Beat potatoes, milk, seasoned salt & 2 tablespoons margarine in a mixing bowl until fluffy.

Mix in sour cream, cream cheese & chives. Turn into buttered casserole dish. Combine remaining tablespoon of margarine with crushed cracker crumbs ~ Sprinkle on top of potato mixture. Bake for 30 minutes in a 350° oven. Top with shredded cheese during last 10 minutes of baking time. ~Serves 5. (This recipe can be prepared a day in advance if you wish.)

Holly's Hint: Eat by candlelight at your next family dinner to make everyone feel special!

19

They'll go **GOOFY** over **HAM·IT· UP LOAF**

1½ lb. ground ham

1 lb. ground pork, unseasoned

1 c. soft bread crumbs

¼ c. onion, finely chopped

¼ c. green pepper *chopped*

2 eggs, beaten

¼ c. milk

1 T. prepared mustard

Combine all ingredients in a large mixing bowl. Form mixture into a loaf. Place in ungreased loaf pan. Set aside.

● Now fix this Glaze ●

10¾ oz. can condensed tomato soup

1 c. brown sugar

½ c. pineapple juice

1 t. dry mustard

Blend ingredients in saucepan 'til smooth. Simmer glaze for 5 minutes over low heat. Spoon it over ham loaf 'til top is completely covered. (Serve any remaining glaze, warm, alongside cooked ham loaf)

Bake at 350° for 1 to 1½ hours.

Sure to be a family favorite... a great POTLUCK dish!

SERVE UP A LITTLE FUN

with Your Meal!

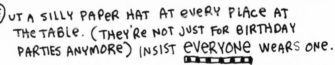

"Always laugh when you can. It's cheap Medicine." ~ Lord Byron

PUT A SILLY PAPER HAT AT EVERY PLACE AT THE TABLE. (THEY'RE NOT JUST FOR BIRTHDAY PARTIES ANYMORE) INSIST <u>EVERYONE</u> WEARS ONE.

INVITE YOUR FAVORITE CARTOONS TO SUPPER — USE THE FUNNY PAPERS FOR PLACEMATS OR FOR A COLORFUL TABLE COVER.

HIDE THE GOOD CHINA AND SET THE TABLE WITH BRIGHT YELLOW PAPER PLATES, ORANGE NAPKINS & PURPLE PAPER CUPS — OR ANY OTHER EYE-POPPING COLOR COMBINATIONS!

MAKE <u>HAPPY</u> HAM LOAF (FOR PICKY EATERS): BAKE MINI-LOAVES AND USE TWO MARASCHINO CHERRY-HALVES FOR EYES & A HALF OF A PINEAPPLE RING FOR A SMILE.

DRESS FOR DINNER — EVERYBODY MUST SPORT AN UGLY TIE!

PLAY FUN MUSIC AND **S**ING ALONG LOUDLY.

21

A RECIPE FROM
THE KITCHEN OF
Mary Elizabeth

Heavenly
Macaroni & Cheese

Dear
Friends —
This recipe
is so good! It is
truly a "comfort" food
warm and filling.

— Mary
Elizabeth

Mary Elizabeth's
recipes

22

Heavenly Macaroni and Cheese

1½ c. small elbow macaroni
1 T. onion, finely chopped
3 T. margarine
2 T. flour
½ t. dry mustard

½ t. salt
⅛ t. pepper
dash cayenne pepper
2 c. milk
2 c. sharp American cheese, cubed

Topping :   6 slices of tomato
1½ c. soft bread crumbs   2 T. margarine, melted

Cook macaroni according to package directions; drain and set aside. Cook onion in margarine 'til tender but not brown. Add flour, mustard, salt & peppers. Stir to form a paste. Add milk all at once to flour mixture. Cook, stirring constantly 'til mixture is thickened.

Add cubed cheese and continue stirring 'til cheese is completely melted. Pour over macaroni & blend well. Place in a buttered casserole dish and arrange tomato slices on top. Toss bread crumbs w/ melted margarine & sprinkle on top. Bake 30 minutes in 350° oven.

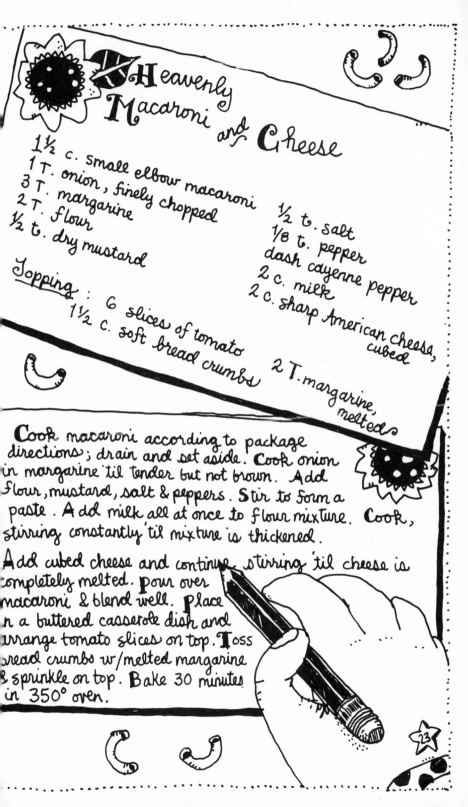

23

The car got stuck in a snowdrift.

You lost one of your mittens.

It was a 2-mile hike back to the phone in your tennis shoes.

You finally got home and remembered you locked your keys back in the car.

It started to sleet.

Your day went down-hill from there.

THE I·Had·a· ReeeAllY· Rough· Day· dinner.

SUPPER TIME!

OK. Here's what you do.

#1 Put on Your flannel, Jammies. (the real soft wrinkly polka-dot ones)

#2 Slip into your fuzzy-bunny Slippers.

③ Fix tHis,

Tomato Basil Soup

2 c. chicken broth
½ c. onion, finely chopped
¼ c. celery, finely chopped
6 med. tomatoes —
    peeled, seeded & chopped
¼ t. dried basil, crushed
2 t. sugar   2 t. flour
2 T. butter or margarine
1 c. milk   salt & pepper

Combine broth, onion, celery, 3/4 of chopped tomatoes, basil & sugar in a saucepan. Bring to a boil. Cover & reduce heat ~ simmer 15 minutes. In a blender or food processor, puree tomato mixture in small batches 'til smooth. Set aside. In same saucepan, melt butter and lightly cook remaining tomatoes. Blend in flour, salt & pepper. Add milk all at once. Cook over low heat 'til thick & bubbly. Stir in pureed tomato mixture ~ heat through (do not boil) and serve. Makes 4 bowls.

"The smell of Basil is good for the HEART & HEAD, and maketh a man MERRY & GLAD."
    - Old Proverb -

#4 Eat it.

#5 Wrap up in a quilt in front of the fire.
Take Spotty and a 1-lb chocolate bar with you.

#6 Call your two best friends in the whole·wide·world for a little SYMPATHY.

Now, isn't it all better?

OtHeR WAYS to FeeL HAPPieR:

♥ Get into a WARM BATH ~ use Lots of bubbles. ♥ Turn off all the lights and read a steamy novel by candle-glow. ♥ Get out your old PHOTO ALBUMS and look at Spotty's baby pictures. ♥ Paint your toenails fire-engine red. ♥ Sprinkle lavender-scented TALCUM POWDER on your sheets and go to sleep. Tomorrow is another day!

End·of·the day·and·I'm· too·lazy·to cook·dinner

You've been out in the garden all afternoon. You're hot. You're sunburned. A big meal is too much to contemplate cooking or eating.

So what's for Supper?

Best·ever Grilled Cheese Sandwich

FOR ONE SANDWICH, USE:

- ½ t. Dijon mustard
- 1 T. mayonnaise
- 2 thick slices of Sourdough bread
- butter
- Slice of swiss cheese
- Slice of cheddar cheese
- 1 to 2 slices tomato
- thin slice of red onion
- 3 slices of bacon, cooked

Mix mustard and mayonnaise together ~ spread on one slice of bread. Top with cheeses, onion, tomato, bacon and other bread slice. Spread butter on outer sides of bread. Place on griddle or frying pan. Toast on both sides on low heat, flipping sandwich over 'til cheese is melted and bread is golden brown.

27

Better to idle Well than to Work badly. — Spanish Proverb

CLASSIC Veggie Soup

Holly's 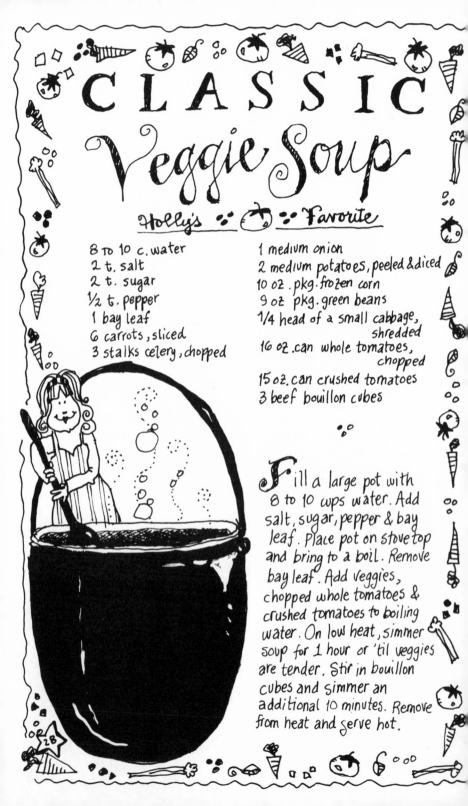 Favorite

8 to 10 c. water
2 t. salt
2 t. sugar
½ t. pepper
1 bay leaf
6 carrots, sliced
3 stalks celery, chopped

1 medium onion
2 medium potatoes, peeled & diced
10 oz. pkg. frozen corn
9 oz. pkg. green beans
1/4 head of a small cabbage, shredded
16 oz. can whole tomatoes, chopped
15 oz. can crushed tomatoes
3 beef bouillon cubes

Fill a large pot with 8 to 10 cups water. Add salt, sugar, pepper & bay leaf. Place pot on stovetop and bring to a boil. Remove bay leaf. Add veggies, chopped whole tomatoes & crushed tomatoes to boiling water. On low heat, simmer soup for 1 hour or 'til veggies are tender. Stir in bouillon cubes and simmer an additional 10 minutes. Remove from heat and serve hot.

28

Dried Herbs

Such as basil, thyme, marjoram or rosemary can be added to veggie soup for a little more zip. Start by adding 1/4 teaspoon of the chosen herb ⌒ allow it to simmer in broth for 10 minutes, then sample the broth.

Remember ⌒ it's easier to add more than it is to subtract! Herbs should enhance the flavor of the dish, not overpower it.

Holly

'Worries go down better with Soup than without.'
— Jewish Proverb

EVEN NON-TUNA-LOVERS WILL FALL HOOK, LINE & SINKER FOR THIS CREAMY CASSEROLE!

iNGREDiENTS:

8 oz. PACKAGE MEDIUM NOODLES
3 T. BUTTER or MARGARINE
½ c. CELERY, FINELY CHOPPED
⅓ c. ONION, FINELY CHOPPED
¼ c. CARROT, FINELY CHOPPED
         OR SHREDDED

2 T. FLOUR
2 c. MILK

4 oz. CREAM CHEESE
1 c. AMERICAN CHEESE, CUBED
6½ oz. CAN TUNA, DRAINED
½ t. SALT
¼ t. PEPPER
1 c. CRUSHED POTATO CHIPS

COOK NOODLES ACCORDING TO PACKAGE DIRECTIONS. DRAIN AND SET ASIDE.

MELT BUTTER IN A SAUCEPAN, AND ADD CELERY, ONION & CARROT ⌒ COOK 'TIL TENDER BUT NOT BROWN.

STIR IN FLOUR UNTIL A PASTE IS FORMED.

ADD MILK ALL AT ONCE ⌒ COOK & STIR UNTIL MIXTURE IS THICKENED AND BUBBLY.

ADD CREAM & AMERICAN CHEESES, STIRRING 'TIL COMPLETELY MELTED.

FOLD TUNA, SALT, PEPPER & COOKED NOODLES INTO CHEESE SAUCE MIXTURE, AND PLACE MIXTURE IN A BUTTERED CASSEROLE DISH.

SPRINKLE WITH CRUSHED POTATO CHIPS.

BAKE 30 MINUTES IN A 350° OVEN. ⌒ SERVES 5

Main Dish Collection Index

"Since Eve ate Apples, much depends on dinner."

~ Lord Byron, "Don Juan"